Let Me Be FREE

Lanae S. Taylor

Let Me Be Free

By: Lanae S. Taylor

Cover Photo by: F and Y Photography

Cover Compiled by: Jazzy Kitty Publishing

Logo Designs by: Andre M. Saunders/Leroy Grayson

Photographs: F and Y Photography and Photobucket.com

Editor: Anelda L. Attaway

© 2018 Lanae S. Taylor

ISBN 978-0-9988433-7-7

Library of Congress Control Number: 2017961421

All rights reserved. This book is protected under the copyright laws of the United States of America. This book may not be copied or reprinted for commercial gain or profit. The use of short quotations or occasional page copying for personal use or group study is permitted and encouraged. Permission will be granted upon request. For Worldwide Distribution, available in Paperback. Printed in the United States of America. Published by Jazzy Kitty Publishing, LLC. Utilizing Microsoft Publishing Software.

ACKNOWLEDMENTS

I would like to thank, first and foremost, God for allowing this opportunity to present itself in my path. I believe that everything happens for a reason.

I thank all of my closest friends and family for sticking by me and supporting me while this book was in the works.

I would like to thank my wonderful photographer, Frank Holmes of F and Y Photography for my beautiful book cover and bio photos.

To my dearest friend who passed, the late Mr. English-I would like to thank you for always motivating me and providing the confidence I needed to even think about publishing my poetry. My only wish was that I would be able to tell you about my accomplishment in person.

To my sister friend, Crystal Johnson, thank you for seeing my potential and pointing me in the direction of a fabulous publisher.

Of course, I want to thank my fabulous publisher Anelda Attaway of Jazzy Kitty Publishing for all the guidance and publishing this great successful book (speaking it into existence!).

And if you are reading this, I would like to give a special thank you for purchasing my book and I hope you enjoy it!

MY SPECIAL DEDICATION

I dedicate this book to my sister C. Sharon "Coco" Taylor, my ride or die, and my rock. She is not only my sister, but she is my friend, my comedian, my confidant, and when needed, my shoulder to cry on. She has been there for me, throughout it all, and when I felt like giving up, she was right there to push me further.

TABLE OF CONTENTS

INTRODUCTION i

LIFE **01**

    Being Black 03

    Assumptions-Being Black (Part 2) 06

    My Life is a Sad Song 10

    Struggles of Life 14

LOVE **17**

    Being Together 18

    Best Kept Secret 20

    Special Love 22

    Mission Possible 25

    My Complete Life 28

CHANGE **29**

    Bleeding Heart 31

    Oh, How I Missed You 35

    Speechless 36

    Torn 38

    Entrapment 41

    Waiting 44

LUST **46**

    All I Want Is You 47

    Taken 50

    Loving My Man 54
FREEDOM...**56**
    Waiting for You 58
    Just Write.. 61
    Let Me Be 64
ABOUT THE AUTHOR **66**

INTRODUCTION

This book of poetry is a collection of life's emotional roller coaster that one could have ridden on, or have mentally put themselves through the ups and downs. Sometimes you want revenge, sometimes you let karma take care of it, while other times you just want to scream in rage. Just take a peaceful moment to breathe in and exhale out; then tell them. . . just LET ME BE FREE.

Let Me Be Free

LIFE

Lanae S. Taylor

BEING BLACK

**BEING BLACK CAN BE WISE,
AS IF BLACK WAS AN OWL**

BEING BLACK

BEING BLACK can be Beautiful,
As if Black was a Flower

BEING BLACK can be Wise,
As if Black was an Owl

BEING BLACK can be Graceful,
As if Black was a Swan

Black. Stop. Think.
Who are you?

Beautiful, Wise, Graceful, Black?
I know . . . 'Cause I am too

Just a kid in School,
Much to struggle for
Trying to have a Future,
Trying to get Ahead,
Trying to accomplish Goals,

Trying to make a Change,

For the Beautiful People;

For the Wise People;

For the Graceful People

All Confidence

All Determination

Wishing for Success

Just being Myself,

Just being a **STRONG BLACK WOMAN**

ASSUMPTIONS~ BEING BLACK

JUST A BLACK FEMALE,
WITH A LOT TO PROVE WRONG
MAKING SURE THESE ASSUMPTIONS
DON'T GET TO ME
TRYING TO ALWAYS STAY STRONG

ASSUMPTIONS~ BEING BLACK
(PART 2)

BEING BLACK.

Female.

Focused without a He.

Right now, it's just all about Me

Why do people **ASSUME?**

Even before I was in My Mother's Womb

ASSUMING,

I cannot be Educated

My Thirst for Knowledge

Has NEVER Faded

ASSUMING,

I do not have Strength

Dealing with Complexity

Through Life's Length

ASSUMING,

I CANNOT take Care of Oneself

Man Please, Really?

I'm already by Myself

BLACK.

FEMALE.

Stop.

Think.

Who am I, Really?

I am Who?

Educated, Strong, Independent?

Mmmm Hmmm 'Cause I'm Amazing,

Beautiful and Sassy TOO

Just a **BLACK FEMALE**,

With a Lot to Prove Wrong

Making sure these **ASSUMPTIONS** don't get to Me

Trying to Always Stay Strong

For the Educated Me;

For the Strong Me;

For the Independent Me

Wishing there was No Color

No Judgment,

No **ASSUMPTIONS**

Seeing Me for Me

Just being Myself

Proving **ASSUMPTIONS** Wrong

As I Cannot and Will Not Change who I am

JUST BEING A BLACK WOMAN, STRONG

MY LIFE IS A SAD SONG

NO ONE REALLY TAKES THE TIME TO SIT DOWN,
AND HELP SORT OUT THE PROBLEMS,
THE DEPRESSION, THE MISSING PIECES
TO THE PUZZLE OF MY LIFE

Lanae S. Taylor

MY LIFE IS A SAD SONG

MY LIFE IS A SAD SONG;
And so are the people in it
It seems every time I am Happy
There is Always someone there
To bring Tears of Sadness

I know I should Avoid people like that
But it seems I Attract those Negative people
The "WORLD" claims those who
Attract Negative are Negative themselves

I try to be Positive but still with Trying
LIFE IS A SAD SONG

The "WORLD" claims it is a Sign of Maturity
When you Sort out your Feelings
Know your Rights from Wrongs,
And Learn and Understand your Mistakes
So, you won't do them again

Let Me Be Free

I feel Mature . . .

But sometimes NOT Mature Enough

When I want to be

I need Someone to Understand me

Know Me and Most of all, Love Me

And then they will Understand

Why I Do what I Do

The "WORLD" won't let the Man I Love, Love Me

I am NOT suppose to know what Love is

Or show it as the "WORLD" claims,

But a Girl Can Dream

No one really takes the Time to Sit Down,

And help Sort out the Problems,

The Depression, the Missing Pieces

To the Puzzle of **MY LIFE**

I miss So Much and know So Little

The "WORLD" won't Sit Down

But they sure can Stand Up

And Knock Me Down

I try to be Strong, but I NEED someone

To Support Me to be Stronger,

So, I CANNOT be Knocked Down

Or even Moved

No one Cares. . .

At least, if someone Actually Cared

Then the "WORLD" would not

Be Claiming all the Time,

They would be Listening

That could be the Reason Why

MY LIFE IS A SAD SONG

STRUGGLES OF LIFE

I WOULD WANT TO SAY,
I SEE LIFE FULL OF BEAUTIFUL THINGS
SUNSHINY DAYS
AND ALL OF THE JOY IT BRINGS

BUT THAT WOULD BE NOTHING BUT LIES
BECAUSE YOU ARE NOT VIEWING LIFE
FROM MY EYES

STRUGGLES OF LIFE

I would want to say,

I see Life FULL of Beautiful things

Sunshiny Days and All of the Joy It Brings

But that would be Nothing but Lies

Because you are NOT Viewing Life

From My Eyes

I see Mothers **STRUGGLING** to Raise their Children

Like our Parents did so long ago back then

But getting by on Minimum Wage

With no Benefits and only Rage

Towards the Fathers that are in Jail

Forcing the Mothers to stay Focus and don't Fail

I see these Streets are Killing our Kids

With Drugs, Gangs, and More

They are not even Paying Attention

To the many Opportunities and the Open Doors

With what used to be a Joy and Glory

Now becomes a Survival

And a Sad Story

I see Discrimination . . .

Boy its not Easy being Black

Never has been and Proving these Whack

Ignorant People that we can Become

So much More, Forget that, BEING DUMB

We are great Leaders and Teachers

With beautiful Cocoa Skin

And Dark Features

Even with all the Sadness, the Struggles, the Defeat

We all tend to STILL Smile

And Take a Front Seat

On this Ride that we are Strapped in

Taking every Bump, Twist and Turn to Win

At this Game we call Life and Living in the Hood

Fighting the Battle to get OUT if we Could

I would want to Say,

I see life FULL of Beautiful things

Sunshiny Days and All of the Joy It Brings

But that would be Nothing but Lies

Because you are NOT Viewing Life from My Eyes

LOVE

Lanae S. Taylor

BEING TOGETHER

Each Day that we Shared

Shows that we both Care about Each Other

When times get Hard and things get Difficult,

We both come **TOGETHER** as a Whole

I Stand by You, as you by Me

There are times like This when we are

NOT TOGETHER

Which makes Me Think of you More

Until we are together Once Again,

The Love, in which we have

Combined together as One,

Will ALWAYS be in our Hearts

Especially when we are Thinking of Each other

And NOT being able to **COME TOGETHER**

At that Moment

BEST KEPT SECRET

IS MY SECRET SAFE WITH YOU?
AM I YOUR SECRET TOO?
JUST SINFUL WITH MY EMOTIONS,
LIKE EVE AND THAT POISONED APPLE
DON'T KNOW WHAT TO DO,
FEELING LIKE STAINED GLASS,
PRISTINE AND FRAGILE

BEST KEPT SECRET

Don't Speak, Don't Open your Mouth . . .

Don't Say Another Word

That Knowledge you were Spittin'

My Mind Thirsty, Absorbing what I Heard

You were never Supposed to have Me,

SECRETLY becoming Yours

Invading Space Once Occupied

Unlocking those Intimate Doors

Is My **SECRET** Safe with You?

Am I your **SECRET** Too?

Once you Stimulated My Mind,

You knew My Body Would Follow

Trying not to Show any Weakness,

Or Appear Too Selfish, too Greedy or Shallow

All these Feelings that was kept Hidden,

Now Pouring out of My Veins like Fine Wine,

The Feelings I have will NEVER Disappear,

Does it mean My Heart Has Crossed the Line?

Is My **SECRET** Safe with you?

Am I Your **SECRET** Too?

Just Sinful with My Emotions,

Like Eve and that Poisoned Apple

Don't know What to Do,

Feeling like stained Glass, Pristine, and Fragile

Is My **SECRET** still Safe with you?

Have I Remained Your **SECRET** Too?

Now I know, it was you all along that I Needed,

Just know you are My **BEST KEPT SECRET**

I will Always and Forever

Love you . . . **SECRETLY**

Lanae S. Taylor

SPECIAL LOVE

I don't know how many Times

You have said I Love You,

But Today, it is like I FELT your LOVE

It could be that

I am Finally Realizing how

SPECIAL OUR LOVE is

It has been Almost a Year

A year of Caring and Sharing,

Loving and Belonging,

Togetherness but also Individuality

We have done More over the Year

Than I EVER Imagined

We have said our Words,

Spoke our Opinions

And even had Disputable Arguments

But we cannot Stay Away from Each other,

Whether we are Happy or Sad

I Daydream about our Moments

And I see, each time it gets Better

I just Hope you will

NEVER STOP Loving ME

Because I will

NEVER STOP Loving YOU

MISSION POSSIBLE

SWEETNESS, JUICY, DELICIOUS,
OH, HOW I NEVER TASTED SOMETHING SO FINE
WISH I COULD BOTTLED IT, SEAL IT
LET IT AGE, LIKE A BOTTLE OF FERMENTED WINE

MISSION POSSIBLE

LOVE IS . . . A MISSION

That holds Loyalty and Trust

Set Forth with no Deadline, NO Rush,

Has anyone Seen it, Felt it, Tasted it?

It can make Me Giggle and Blush

Forgetting about My Messed-up Past

Keeping Me Focused on My Future

And Making this thing we call Love Last

Sweetness, Juicy, Delicious,

Oh, How I NEVER Tasted Something So Fine

Wish I could Bottled it, Seal it

Let it Age, like a Bottle of Fermented Wine

This is Definitely **A MISSION . . . POSSIBLE**

Love is . . . Blind, Never see it, it is just There

Love is . . . Deaf, the Mind doesn't want to Hear

Love is . . . Happiness, a Smile, a Joy to Feel

Love is . . . As Erotic as the Arch in My Heel

Love is . . . The Feeling of Chills, Goosebumps, Hives

Who would have Known

I would have been AFRAID to Open My Eyes

Why don't you make an Appearance?

Show Me that you are Near

So, I can STOP Dreaming, Looking, Searching

For this THING called Love

We BOTH know is There

This is . . . **A MISSION POSSIBLE**

MY COMPLETE LIFE

YOU ARE MY LIFESAVER

KEEPING ME AFLOAT

MY COMPLETE LIFE

When days Go by

That we Aren't able to Share

Special Time Together

I begin to Notice things in **MY LIFE**

AREN'T COMPLETE

You are **MY LIFESAVER** keeping Me Afloat

You are My Laughter keeping Me Smiling

You are My Sunlight that Awakens Me in the Morning

You are My Heart

Which is WHY I Love You So Much

You are the MISSING Ingredient in My Recipe

Until we Reunite Once Again,

Reality just won't Taste the Same

CHANGE

Lanae S. Taylor

BLEEDING HEART

**HEARTS HAVE BEEN BROKEN, CRUSHED,
NO FEELINGS, VERY NUMB
LOOKING FOR HEALING,
PRAYERS TO FADE AWAY
THE SORROW THAT HAS COME**

BLEEDING HEART

Hearts have been Broken, Crushed,

No Feelings, Very Numb

Looking for Healing, Prayers to Fade Away

The Sorrow that has Come

Eyes Swollen like the Full Moon

IS BLEEDING,

Tears Flow, Providing the Earth's

Suggested Feeding

Creating Ponds of Fear, Pools of Hurt

And Puddles of Sadness

Dry your Tears, My Dear Queen,

Soak up the Dampness

We look toward God

For Guidance and Existence

Not to Worry . . .

As a King is within grabbing Distance

Lanae S. Taylor

Waiting for the Moon, Clouds,
And Sorrow to Fade Away
Put the Heart Back Together
By Brightening the Day

When Thoughts that there were No Hope,
Nothing left to Give
The Darkness in the Soul Dissipated
And Gives reasons to Live

Sun Shining, Casting Heat upon a Moist
And Wet Face
Then there was you, a Marvelous Man,
Offering a Safe Place

For Smiles, Kisses, Lust
And Love to Bestow
Making the Sky Blue Again,
Watching as the Grass begins to Grow

Then there was you,

A Gentleman, A Godsend, A King,

Bowing Down, Conquering your Queen,

Offering a Ring

The Full Moon Disappears, Clouds Vanish,

And Sorrow Finally Fades away

Bandage and Mend a **BROKEN HEART**

By Uplifting the Day

Giving oneself as a Nubian Queen,

A Stronger Woman and a Mother of his Seeds

Faithful, Loyal, and Dedicated,

I am Sincerely, all he Needs

A Full Moon and Clouds Will Reappear

But Tears stay Away

With Shielded Hearts,

The Twosome always will have a Beautiful Day

Building on a Dream, a TRUE Vision,

An Empire, a Life NEVER Dim

We thank God every day

For Providing such a Man,

A King like Him

OH, HOW I MISSED YOU

Only you Know How My Heart Cries out for you

Having this Short Separation

Is Tearing Me Apart

And On this Day

I want you to Know how much

I MISSED YOU

And Wish you were Here to Give Me

The Intimacy in which I Yearn for

Many Days have Past

And I have NOT told you

How Sensual you have Made Me Feel

Being your Special Lady

Showing you Care and Love Me

Expressing your Emotions which you have

Deep inside your Heart

AND ULTIMATELY, I HAVE MISSED YOU!

Lanae S. Taylor

SPEECHLESS

All the Words in the World
Could NEVER Express the way I Feel about you
The Care and Respect You Give
Makes Me Feel Special and Unique

The Emotions which I feel Every Day
Are getting Stronger
This is the Special Kind of Love
I Need and Want to Hold on To

I Feel SO Wonderful and Happy
When I'm with you
You Give Me that Rush of Excitement

I Dream about You and Me
Making what we have Something Even Better
I think I have Become
A Different Kind of Woman

I have Learned to Appreciate you

And your Love

I Learned how to Make You Happy

Put a Smile upon your Face

Not a Day goes by

That I don't Think about you

With My Emotions Feelings

Running So High,

Things then, just become **SPEECHLESS**

Lanae S. Taylor

TORN

Tearing . . . Ripping . . . Stripping . . .

The Special Bond, the Growing Emotions

Nothing to Heal the Broken Heart

No Tape, No Glue, No Potions

Speechless . . . Heartbroken . . . Numb . . .

Feelings are Gone, Vanished, just Disappeared

Not wanting to Talk or Listen

All the Inevitable are Feared

No More Hugs . . . No More Lessons . . .

No More Time . . . Just Regret . . .

When I Needed your Guidance the Most,

I'm Scared, Entangled in a Net

But I allowed you with the Memories, the Years,

To Fade . . . Too Quickly, You See

From Birth to 23 . . .

Was Definitely NOT enough for Me

You just don't know how much I Truly Miss you
And your Knowledge on
What true Kings is Supposed to Do

I will NEVER Forget you;
You will Always be My Number One King,
No matter what Man decides to Grace My Finger
With a Lifetime Ring

My Soul will be Lifted but Never Re-born
He will Always know that My Heart was once Stripped
And Completely **TORN**

ENTRAPMENT

**BOY YOU GOT ME ALL CAUGHT UP
I DON'T WANT TO BE ANYWHERE ELSE
BUT IN THIS WEB OF
A DANGEROUS ENTRAPMENT**

ENTRAPMENT

My Mind can't be Exempted,

Thoughts are Constantly Entangled,

Your body Hypnotizing Me…

I can't Break Free

I need to be Released

Somehow, I Don't want to Go

Can't Focus, Can't Think,

So Venerable

Boy you got Me ALL Caught up

In this Dangerous **ENTRAPMENT**

The Intensity of the Eroticism

The Pain in your Pleasure

The Tease of your Lips

The Forcefulness of your Hips

Bites and Nibbles

Arches and Grips

Trembles and Shakes

Ravishing My Whole Body

Blinded but yet Aware

Boy, you just don't Know

You got Me ALL Caught up

In this Dangerous **ENTRAPMENT**

I'm an Endangered Species

Wanting to Step Out

Been in Your Captivity

Your Sheltered Zone, Your Security

My One Only

Feasting off Your Affection

Craving for More

Looking through the Cloud

You have Me Floating On

No one to Save Me,

Catch Me, Break My Fall

Only you are There

My Warrior, My Protector, My Dominator

You are NOT willing to Let Go

Boy you got Me ALL Caught up

I don't want to be anywhere Else

But in this Web of a Dangerous **ENTRAPMENT**

Lanae S. Taylor

WAITING

When I First saw you,

I knew something Special

Was going to Happen in My Life

A Change for the Better,

Something New, Something Different

When you Entered My Life

You Opened Doors that some

Would not even Attempt to Open

You are Encouraging, Caring

Important to Me

For once, I can say I am In Love,

A Love that would Last

Longer than a Lifetime

And would Grow every day of every Year

I want to Express the Love and Care

That I Have for you

And the same I want you to Express

But we know in this Present time and Day

We can ONLY do So Much

But we know if we **WAIT**

We will be There for Each Other

Because our Love is that Strong

LUST

ALL I WANT IS YOU

When will you get to Hold Me Again?

So, Tightly in your Grip

Got Me Going CRAZY over Here

Reminiscing . . . MMM, Biting My Lip

Boi, you NEED to Get to Me

Fast in a Hurry,

You know Where I will Be

So, what do you Plan to Do?

All this Love I have

ALL I WANT . . . IS YOU

I Greet you, Half Naked with a Hot Juicy Kiss

Long and Wet . . .

Telling you that you have been Missed

Then as I Melt in your Warm Embrace

You're Gripping My Ass,

Wearing Panties made of Lace

I have been Waiting, Craving,

Anticipating, Saving

So, what do you Plan to Do?

All this Love I Have

ALL I WANT . . . IS YOU

Looking into your Eyes, the Intensity is There

I know you Want Me

And I am Glad you are Here

I have been Waiting, Craving,

Anticipating, Saving

So, what do you Plan to Do?

All this Love I Have

ALL I WANT . . . IS YOU

We can't Go On like This,

Got Me GOING CRAZY

You need to Make a Move

And Stop being Lazy

I have been Waiting, Craving,

Anticipating, Saving

So, what do you Plan to Do?

All this Love I Have

ALL I WANT . . . IS YOU

Lanae S. Taylor

TAKEN

Feeling Tense . . . Stepping In . . . Eyes Closed
Needing to Release, Back Arched, Body Posed

Nothing but the Warmth of the Water,
Dripping down, Between My Cheeks,
And his Lips positioned on the Arch of My Back,
Playing Hide and Go Seek

As I Lather our entire Bodies,
He quickly **TAKES** over the Rest,
Massaging and Caressing the Roundness
Of My Succulent Breasts

Craving, wanting a Nipple to Placed
Upon his Tempting Lips
Pulling Me Closer,
Holding Me Tightly around My Hips

The Water is Slowly Washing away

The Lustful Kisses that have been Laid

Upon My Caramel Skin

He Pushes Me against the Cold Tile,

Props My Leg up,

Oh Yes Lawd! He is about to Commit a Sin

Legs Spread just enough to Handle the Triangle

Without being led Astray

Gripping My Ass, Pulling Me Towards him,

Tasting My Sweetness, Sucking My Soul Away

All I can do is Clutch his Head,

Holding on, Using both Hands

His Tongue, My Hips, Dancing to the Rhythm,

No Need for Commands

He got Me Biting My Lip, Scratching his Back,

Gasping for Air, It Feels So Good,

This was all a Language

Definitely My Body Understood
Letting out a Moan, Sigh, and then a Scream,
He Begs Me to Flood him with My Caramel Cream

Now its time, for Me to Reciprocate,
Water Lukewarm now,
Bouncing off his Chocolate Frame

The way he just Satisfied Me,
The Temperature is Far from anyone's Blame

Can't wait to Wrap My Lips
Around his Thick Milk Chocolate Stick,
As I Love the way it Expands and he Sighs,
At the Touch of My Tongue's First Lick

Now, I get to take him Deep
In My Warm Mouth, Firm, Tightness,
His Stick disappears as he Watches
Me **TAKE** care of Business

I can tell he Adores My Mouth, the Sounds,
My Tongue, Grabbing My Head, Thrusting his Stick
Boi, are you Sprung?

Inch by Inch . . . Thrust by Thrust
He can't take it Anymore
I need him Inside of Me,
But I want to Taste him, Certainly, For sure

Pleasure, Release, Relief . . .
We are both still in Amazement and Disbelief

How I can make his Stick Ooze of Milk Chocolate
Oh, How I Crave that Milk to Hit
My Tongue, Throat, and Palate

Water Flowing, Totally Cold . . .
Skin is Wrinkle, Looking Old
But Definitely feeling Tamed . . .
Eyes Open with My Body FULLY Proclaimed

LOVING MY MAN

To Make Love to **MY MAN**
No One can tell you Better than I Can

It's like we are on a Deserted Island
All Alone, giving each other
The Pleasure were both been Waiting for

Those Soft Erotic Kisses
That Leaves Me Breathless is
Moistened by the Touch of our Tongues

Nothing on Our Minds
Except the Love we have for Each Other

His Wet, Moistened Tongue
Goes Slowly Down My Body
The Shivers he sends Me Through
Goes Quickly Up My Body

My Body is Hot and Wet

And so is his

Messages in My Body

Tells Me it's Time

To Make Love to **MY MAN**

As we Lay Down together,

I feel his Manhood Rise

As we Rock to the same Rhyme,

We make our Own Music

To feel all of **MY MAN** inside of Me,

The Feeling of Ecstasy will NEVER Stop

As we Reach our Climaxes,

I hold Him, he holds Me,

We Relax and then it Starts All Over Again

It is Great to Make Love to **MY MAN**

Lanae S. Taylor

FREEDOM

WAITING FOR YOU

NOW THE TIME IS ALMOST NEAR,
FOR US TO BE WHOLE AGAIN,
I AM COUNTING THE DAYS,
THE HOURS, THE MINUTES . . .

WAITING FOR YOU

WAITING for Anything feels like a Lifetime

But **WAITING FOR YOU**

Seems to be an Eternity

I'm Glad you have Given Me Something Special

As a Reason to **WAIT FOR YOU** . . .

You have Given Me Love,

Love that is Sacred and Pure,

Which is why I **WAIT FOR YOU**

You are Sincere,

Showing and Proving your Feelings Are True,

Which is why I **WAIT FOR YOU**

You are a Man who is

A Protector, Provider and Warrior

Which is why I **WAIT FOR YOU**

You are a Man I Believe in

I know you WILL be there for Me

When I Need You Most

Which is why I **WAIT FOR YOU**

Now the Time is almost Near,

For us to be Whole again,

I am Counting the Days, the Hours, the Minutes . . .

I Miss being able to be with you Completely

But I will be Happy when Eternity's Door Opens

And Releases you to Me

Because I don't have a Lifetime

TO WAIT FOR ANYTHING ELSE

JUST WRITE

**FINALLY FIGURED IT OUT,
JUST WRITE WHAT YOU FEEL
GETTING THOSE WORDS OUT,
IT HELPS ME HEAL**

JUST WRITE

Pencil and Paper,

This is How It Began

What do I **WRITE** about?

Just a youngster Then

Love, Life, Changes . . .

In My Mind, Get Outta My Head,

Words Ranges

Got to put these Thoughts on Paper,

Feeling Pressured

Words Dancing Around,

Need to Jump out on this Paper

Love, Life, Changes . . .

In My Mind, Get Outta My Head,

Words Ranges

Now its Pen and Paper

Scared of Expression, Switching Tools

Got to put these Thoughts on Paper,

I feel like a Fool

Love, Life, Changes . . .

In My Mind, Get Outta My Head,

This all Feels Strange

Finally figured it out,

JUST WRITE what you Feel

Getting those Words out,

It helps Me Heal

Love, Life, Changes . . .

NO MORE Pressure

In My Mind, Get Outta My Head,

Words Flow from Pen to on this Paper

LET ME BE . . .

THAT STRONG WOMAN I HAVE GROWN TO BE

RATHER YOU TEAR ME DOWN,

HURT ME AND TRY TO CONTROL ME

Lanae S. Taylor

LET ME BE

LET ME BE . . .

That Strong Woman I have Grown to Be

Rather you Tear Me Down,

Hurt Me and Try to Control Me

Ashamed that I Allowed you to Steal

So much of My Soul and Joy,

Showing Me Off like a Child on Christmas Day

With a Brand-New Toy

I was being Played for a Fool

It took Me a while to Understand

Can't believe you had Me

Eating out the Palm of your Hand

LET ME BE . . . LET ME BE FREE

My Eyes are Wide Open and I See

Exactly what you are Doing to Me

To Love and Honor

Is what you Vowed to God

But what you really were was

A devil in Disguise

All you Provided was Heartache and Pain,

Making Me Feel like I could NEVER Trust

Or Love Another Man

My Faith in God Helped Mend

My Damaged Heart

Because Lord knows I could NOT Pretend

And Play another year's Part

To be able to LOVE AGAIN . . .

LET ME BE . . .

JUST TO BE . . . TO BE FREE

ABOUT THE AUTHOR

Lanae is a native of Philadelphia, PA. In 2004, she uprooted to the Newark-Bear area of Delaware where she now resides after spending five years abroad, in Naples, Italy.

She started writing poetry at the age of 16. However, writing poetry was kept a secret for several years as it was her outlet to relax her mind, body, and soul. It was her way of expression and emotional release.

She is near completion of her Bachelor of Science in Technical Management, with a concentration in Health Management, she holds a perfect 4.0 GPA at DeVry University. She is currently working in the medical billing field but continues to write.

www.ingramcontent.com/pod-product-compliance
Lightning Source LLC
Chambersburg PA
CBHW020430010526
44118CB00010B/514